HAPPY BIRTHDAY

TO

....

WITH LOVE FROM

....

And Liam

HAPPY BIRTHDAY—LOVE . . .
Complete Series

Jane Austen

Joan Crawford

Bette Davis

Liam Gallagher

Audrey Hepburn

John Lennon

Bob Marley

Marilyn Monroe

Michelle Obama

Jackie Kennedy Onassis

Elvis Presley

Keith Richards

Frank Sinatra

Elizabeth Taylor

Oscar Wilde

HAPPY BIRTHDAY

Love, Liam

ON YOUR SPECIAL DAY
ENJOY THE WIT AND WISDOM OF
LIAM GALLAGHER
THE WORLD'S GREATEST HELLRAISER

Edited by Jade Riley

CELEBRATION BOOKS

THIS IS A CELEBRATION BOOK

Published by Celebration Books 2023
Celebration Books is an imprint of Dean Street Press

Text & Design Copyright © 2023 Celebration Books

All Rights Reserved. No part of this publication may be reproduced, stored in or transmitted in any form or by any means without the written permission of the copyright owner and the publisher of this book.

Cover by DSP

ISBN 978 1 915393 58 6

www.deanstreetpress.co.uk

HAPPY BIRTHDAY—LOVE, LIAM

If there's a brasher rock star on the planet, ladies and gentlemen, do point him out. Liam Gallagher, born to Irish Catholic parents in Manchester, England, may have the biggest, funniest and dirtiest mouth in all of popular music. Interestingly, he attributes getting conked on the head with a hammer during a grade school brawl for music suddenly coming into his head. Famous for fighting with his brother, Oasis band mate, Noel, the dueling duo made some of the greatest records of the '90s. Their most successful album *(What's the Story) Morning Glory?* was an international chart topper and remains one of the best selling records of all time. This perhaps helps Liam when he describes his work as better than the Beatles. Rude, cheeky, arrogant are all terms that can be applied to Liam, but he is also a great kidder who readily admits the Beatles were the best. He even named one of his sons Lennon. Speaking of family, Liam has four children with four different ladies, a few conceived while he was married elsewhere. No matter, Liam is a great Dad and gives his kids the freedom and support they need.

Fans of Oasis are well aware that the band broke up in 2009 when Noel Gallagher abruptly left. The tabloids surely missed their antics and were disappointed to hear they were getting on famously at a party chez George Michael. Still, a reunion remains unlikely. Liam went on to form Beady Eye which lasted until 2014, and is now engaged in solo work. At least he has no one left to argue with! With four number one songs, his career is going great but he claims the solo act "is boring as fuck" and he "would much rather be in a band."

Liam was recently paid £500,000 to play for thirty minutes at a party. Odds are; he's still complaining.

Liam Gallagher

Every time I look in the mirror, God looks back.

"Just get out there and do your bit.

"I refuse to dance. And I can't dance anyway. I'm not in a band for that."

"There's no rules. Show me the rule book.

I know how to behave but sometimes I can't be bothered.

I live for now, not for what happens after I die. If I die and there's something afterwards, I'm going to hell, not heaven.

If I did see a politician taking drugs he'd get a crack 'round the head.

If you want to see the opposite sex sprout four heads, then exchange a couple of rings. You walk to the altar with a woman with one head and you walk back with a fucking monster.

I see myself as one of the fucking true great rock'n'roll singers on the planet.

I live for now. Not for what happens after I die.

I'm Liam Gallagher and I'm in Oasis. The whole world is jealous of me. It should be.

There's no one way to bring up a child. Hopefully you use common sense. Let them get on with it. It's their life.

Being a lad is what I'm about. I can tell you who isn't a lad—anyone from Blur.

If you don't like what you're doing, it must be strange.

I'm getting up earlier and earlier now man. I try and beat the alarm clock. The alarm goes off at six and I try to get up at 5.59 just to do its head in.

I've mellowed, but not in the sense of liking Radiohead or Coldplay.

"I'm not looking for guidance."

Chris Martin looks like a geography teacher.

"I'll never have a stylist."

Fifty pounds is too much to be paying for a pair of socks.

I am a tender, beautiful and loving guy that happens to slap a photographer now and then because they get in my way.

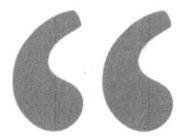
I'm not really keen on sax. I always find it a bit creepy.

"I did fall out of a helicopter, but it was on the ground.

I don't think tension makes for great records. That's a load of bollocks.

"I'm not one of them that walks around town like I'm the king of London. If I need to get milk I go out and get milk, but most of the time I'm indoors.

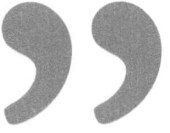

 I was walking along and this chair came flying past me, and another, and another, and I thought, man, is this gonna be a good night.

Everyone knows that if you've got a brother, you're going to fight.

Fuck the sea. I ain't going in that. Fuck that, mate. That ain't meant for us. That's meant for the sharks, and the jellyfish, tadpoles and stuff.

Eat less, move more and don't drink beer—it's as simple as that. But me I love pie and chips—so it's really hard.

I don't think I've ever said anything that's nasty.

I don't know what any of my songs are about. I don't sit down to write about anything. They're about whatever you want. I don't pick subjects. I just start.

I have got a bit of an issue with cardigans. They're shit aren't they?

Rock stars exercising?
I don't think it's right.
You either got it or
you ain't.

"I've been there, bought the T-shirt. If you ever need to have a chat about anything, I'm your man.

I can still go pound for pound with any clown at any time.

The Beatles play guitars, we play guitars. The Beatles got hair, we've got hair. The Beatles got arms, we've got arms.

"New York is my favorite city in the world."

I've got to be by trees, otherwise I get claustrophobic.

 I've never met a bad Virgo.

I love the Beatles. What more can I say? I'm not gonna lie to you. I love 'em. They make me happy. And I think they were the best, and still are.

[On brother Noel]: He's in one of his really, really, really, really, really, really, really, really, really, really big houses. Probably eatin' tofu while havin' a fuckin' face peel, isn't that right, man of the people?

Playing them big concerts, you've got to be match fit. Make sure you get plenty of early nights and look after yourself.

A lot of fears are illusions, so you just have to take a deep breath and think: You know what? It's not that bad actually.

If I lost my hair you would never see me on that stage again, because there's no place for baldness in rock'n'roll.

It's good people living on your doorstep and looking through your bins. Gives you energy.

Americans want grungy people, stabbing themselves in the head on stage. They get a bright bunch like us, with deodorant on, they don't get it.

"I will always be an Oasis."

"Why did I get an Elvis tattoo? Because he's cool."

"I was brought up Catholic. Then I had a joint and looked at the world differently.

"I didn't always want to be a dad.

"

Once the music gets in you, it doesn't leave you.

If someone's barking up the wrong tree I sort of point them in the right direction, but other than that I'm not into tweeting—it's rubbish.

There's Elvis and me. I couldn't say which of the two is best.

"I find words really hard.

Discipline. I don't know the meaning of the word.

You've got to talk a lot of shit to get to the nitty-gritty truth. The more shit you say, the more you get to the absolute point.

I do believe I was supposed to be on a stage singing songs. I've got some good lungs on me.

"Name one rock star in Britain apart from a member of Oasis. Name one!

I'm not like John Lennon, who thought he was the great Almighty. I just think I'm John Lennon.

Noel Gallagher, Russell Brand, fucking hell . . . what a pair of old housewives.

I don't go out and get wasted. I've got kids and they're getting to that age when they're like, 'How come you get to lie in bed all day and I've got to go to school?'

The good times outweigh the bad times. I think it's best to just leave it at that.

"I know how great I am and I know how shit I am."

I dig it. I'm into the idea that there could be a God and aliens and reincarnation and some geezer years ago turning water into wine. I don't believe when you die, you die.

"You've seen one of the our gigs you've seen 'em all.

I'm not sure if I believe in God, but if he's meant to be the main guy and all that tackle, then maybe I'd give him a kick in the bollocks and say: What the fuck are you doing, letting all these young kids get killed in all these wars and stuff?

 I'm into the girls fancying me and stuff, mad for it.

I don't think I've put a foot wrong. I think it's gone pretty much to plan.

Not everyone can say, 'I'm going to write a classic today.' If that was the case, we'd all be doing it.

I fucking hate Glastonbury, mate. I'm only here for the money.

> I sound good.
> I look cool.
> I talk from the heart.

"I'm an average lad who was born in Burnage who played conkers. Conkers, mate. Conkers.

It's a good job I'm not a snowflake.

All good about turning fifty. The longer you're there for, the better it is. I like being alive.

Money changes a lot of people, but it don't change me.

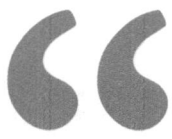

I'd like to be remembered for: He did exactly what it said on the tin. And I looked good while I fucking did it as well.

 I like the Queen—I think she's a little Jedi.

I was never much of a performer, me. I was anti-performance.

"Making music is fucking easy!"

# "I don't mind a little pain. Keeps you on your toes. "

That's the story of my life, mate, I'm always having to go one louder.

"I'd like to think most of us are fucking decent people, but we all have our days when we can be a bit bratty, or ratty or cunty.

We're all going to die, aren't we? Or all we already dead?

I'm afraid of going in the ground and that being it.

Life is there to be loved and lived, you know what I mean?

Turn that fucking shit fog machine off.

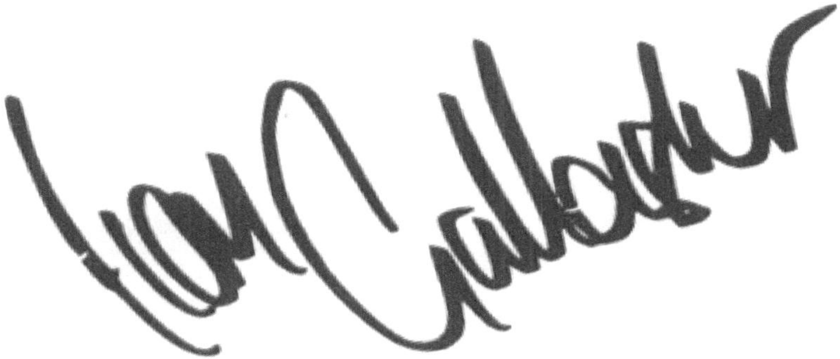

ABOUT THE EDITOR

Jade Riley is a writer whose interests include old movies, art history, vintage fashion and books, books, books.

Her dream is to move to London, to write like Virginia Woolf, and to meet a man like Mr. Darcy, who owns a vacation home in Greece.

www.ingramcontent.com/pod-product-compliance
Lightning Source LLC
Chambersburg PA
CBHW021131130526
44590CB00055B/360